The Early Church
A Study in Acts 1–12

BIBLE STUDIES TO IMPACT THE LIVES OF ORDINARY PEOPLE

The Word Worldwide

by Esma Cardinal

CHRISTIAN
FOCUS

Unless otherwise stated, quotations from the Bible are from the New International Version, © 1973, 1978, 1984 by International Bible Society, published in Great Britain by Hodder and Stoughton Ltd.

ISBN 978-1-84550-816-6

Copyright © WEC International

Published in 2002, reprinted in 2012
by
Christian Focus Publications, Geanies House,
Fearn, Ross-shire, IV20 1TW, Scotland.
www.christianfocus.com
and
WEC International, Bulstrode, Oxford Road,
Gerrards Cross, Bucks, SL9 8SZ.
www.wecinternational.org

Cover design by Daniel van Straaten

Printed and bound by
Bell and Bain, Glasgow

All rights reserved. No part of this publication may be reproduced, stored in a retrieval system, or transmitted, in any form, by any means, electronic, mechanical, photocopying, recording or otherwise without the prior permission of the publisher or a licence permitting restricted copying. In the U.K. such licences are issued by the Copyright Licensing Agency, Saffron House, 6-10 Kirby Street, London, EC1 8TS www.cla.co.uk.

Contents

PREFACE 4
INTRODUCTORY STUDY 5
STUDY 1 7
STUDY 2 10
STUDY 3 13
STUDY 4 16
STUDY 5 19
STUDY 6 22
STUDY 7 25
STUDY 8 28
STUDY 9 31
STUDY 10 34

ANSWER GUIDE
GUIDE TO STUDY 1 37
GUIDE TO STUDY 2 38
GUIDE TO STUDY 3 39
GUIDE TO STUDY 4 40
GUIDE TO STUDY 5 41
GUIDE TO STUDY 6 42
GUIDE TO STUDY 7 43
GUIDE TO STUDY 8 44
GUIDE TO STUDY 9 45
GUIDE TO STUDY 10 46

PREFACE

Where there's LIFE there's GROWTH:
Where there's GROWTH there's LIFE.

WHY GROW a study group?
Because as we study the Bible and share together we can

- learn to combat loneliness, depression, staleness, frustration, and other problems,
- get to understand and love each other,
- become responsive to the Holy Spirit's dealing and obedient to God's Word,

and that's **GROWTH**.

How do you **GROW** a study group?
- Just start by asking a friend to join you and then aim at expanding your group.
- Study the set portions daily (they are brief and easy: no catches).
- Meet once a week to discuss what you find.
- Befriend others, both Christians and non-Christians, and work away together.

see how it **GROWS!**

WHEN you GROW …
This will happen at school, at home, at work, at play, in your youth group, your student fellowship, women's meetings, mid-week meetings, churches and communities,

you'll be **REACHING THROUGH TEACHING.**

WHEN you PRAY…
Remember those involved in writing and producing the study courses, and missionaries and nationals working on the translations into many different languages. Pray that each member of every study group will be enriched personally, and will reach out to involve others. Pray for group leaders and those who direct the studies locally, nationally and internationally.

WHEN you PAY…
All profits from the sale of studies are used to pay translators and to develop the ministry worldwide. May you have the joy of knowing you are working together with those involved in this service.

INTRODUCTORY STUDY

ACTS 1-12

Jerusalem: unfavourable city for a religious revival?
  Crucified carpenter: unsuitable head of a world-wide movement?
  Fishermen: improbable leaders?
  You may think so, without a close look at Acts.

Jesus Christ, Son of the Living God, shines through the pages of this book. He, the main character of the story, is Lord. Sometimes entitled 'The Acts of Jesus Christ' as well as 'The Acts of The Holy Spirit', the book we are studying conveys His Lordship in clear terms.

The author of Acts is Luke. His first letter to Theophilus, 'The Gospel according to Luke', tells what Jesus began to do, while on earth. The second letter, 'The Acts of the Apostles', records what Jesus continued to do, by His Holy Spirit, through the Church. Luke deals chiefly with the expansion of the Church as a whole, paying little attention to the inner life and development of local churches. (Read the Introduction to The Acts of the Apostles in the Good News Bible.)

What is the Church? Such a question must be asked in the light of the whole New Testament. Work through the following acrostic to expand this theme:

Christ's Church is
  Holy Spirit filled,
    United in Him, and
      Redeemed by Him.
        Christians are all
          Heaven-bound.

How did the Church begin? How and why did it spread? Who were its first members? Most importantly, what must we learn today from the Early Church? Our next ten studies in the first twelve chapters of Acts hold some of the answers.

1. Faith in the Saviour, Acts 1.
2. Oneness through the Holy Spirit, Acts 2.
3. Power in Jesus' name, Acts 3.
4. First persecution produces boldness, Acts 4.
5. Willing to suffer, Acts 5.
6. The first martyr forgives, Acts 6 and 7.
7. The first outward move, Acts 8.

8. An enemy becomes an ally, Acts 9.
9. A non-racist gospel, Acts 10 and 11.
10. The Church cannot be destroyed, Acts 12.

Christ alone is the Church's head. Jesus Christ holds all rights to ownership. He is building the Church. See how the following verses acknowledge His authority over the Church. Find other verses on the same theme. Matthew 16:18; Ephesians 4:12,15-16,25; 5:23-24,29,30,32; Colossians 1:18.

The Holy Spirit testifies to Christ, and is God's power in the Church. Before the crucifixion Jesus promised that the Holy Spirit would come. Using these references, discuss why the Holy Spirit is needed: John 14:16-20, 26; 15:26; 16:7, 13-15. Study Two shows how the promise first came true.

Union with Jesus Christ unifies the Church. Because every true believer is joined to Christ, it follows that every true believer is united to all other believers. Apart from Jesus, mankind is fragmented. Do you sense a oneness between Christians? Do these verses provide a reason for your answer to that question? 1 Corinthians 1:2; 6:17; 12:12-27; Ephesians 4:3-6.

Redemption made the Church possible. To redeem is to 'buy back', 'purchase'. Matthew 26:26-29; 1 Corinthians 6:19-20; 7:23; Galatians 3:13; Ephesians 1:7; Colossians 1:13-14; 1 Peter 1:18-19; Revelation 5:9. In these Scripture references look for the need for redemption, and the high price Christ paid. (Some versions of the Bible do not use the words 'redeem' and 'redemption' but you will find the same meaning expressed in other words.) Notice especially the deep significance of the Lord's Supper or Communion.

Christians – all Christians form a part of the Church. That is, every person who receives Christ becomes a child of God and a member of Christ's body. Taking these verses as a sample, try to grasp the wide scope of the Church, from its beginning to the end, reaching to all areas of the earth: John 1:12; 1 Corinthians 1:2; Revelation 5:9; 7:9-10.

Heaven – is the Church's destination. The following references reveal a tiny glimpse of the fantastic future ahead as Christ's bride and co-ruler: Romans 8:17; 1 Corinthians 6:3; Ephesians 3:20-21; Revelation 3:21; 19:7, 9; 21:9.

STUDY 1
FAITH IN THE SAVIOUR

QUESTIONS

DAY 1 Acts 1:1-2; Luke 1:1-4.
a) What had Luke written about in his first book?
What Jesus began to do and teach.

b) How do today's verses encourage you to accept the Bible as true?
Eyewitness accounts – Luke attempting to set things down accurately.

c) When passing on information (written or spoken) do you use the same meticulous care as Luke?
Sometimes – academic background.

DAY 2 Acts 1:3-5; Luke 24:49; 1 Corinthians 15:3-7.
a) How did Jesus spend the six weeks following His death?
Speaking of the kingdom of God, eating.

b) Imagine you had met Him then. What would you have said to Him?
Is it really you and what are you doing here?

c) Why did the apostles need to wait in Jerusalem a for few days?
To receive the Holy Spirit power.

DAY 3 Acts 1:6-11; John 7:39; 16:7; Mark 13:26; 16:19.
a) Give one reason why Jesus must return to heaven and be exalted in this way.
To prove he's the son of God – to send the HS.

b) If the prediction of Acts 1:11 comes true this year, will you be glad or sad?
Scared – confused because the threat of judgement; happy if reunited with dead/redeemed.

scary elements wind, blood, moon, destruction

QUESTIONS (cont.)

DAY 4 Acts 1:8.
a) Discuss with your group how the Christian message came to your area.

b) Whose power sends the gospel throughout the world?
God sends HS to disciples. God empowers D through HS

c) Jerusalem is located in Judea; Samaria is next to Judea. What are the equivalent areas where you live?
Bath e Bristol?

DAY 5 Acts 1:12-14; Matthew 6:7-13.
a) Luke does not tell us what they prayed about in Acts 1:14. Make a short list of their most likely prayer topics.
Understanding why Jesus left - grief? Waiting for God. Trying to work out what to do? Supporting one another

b) Should we, today, follow the guidelines Jesus gave in Matthew 6:7-13?
Yes - don't show off, be honest

DAY 6 Acts 1:15-26; Matthew 26:47-49; John 12:1-6.
a) We feel shocked by Judas' actions. What warnings does his story hold for you?
Don't steal, be mean hearted? Betray self. I thought he hanged himself doesn't sound - though mild Jesus

b) To fill the vacancy as apostle, what two qualifications were needed?
To have been with Jesus the whole time & to have witnessed his resurrection.

DAY 7 Acts 1:14b; John 7:2-5.
a) See how Jesus' half-brothers have changed! Where do you belong: in John 7:5 or Acts 1:14?
Don't know.

b) From Luke 24:45-53 choose at least one vital phrase that has a connection with Acts 1. Share with your group what it means to you.
witnesses - Luke as a writer, disciples appointed someone as witness, being empowered to be witnesses. to Jesus life, death.

NOTES

'Jesus Christ is Lord!' The theme fills every section of this first chapter of Acts. Right from the beginning the writer makes Jesus the Head, as preparations are made for the beginning of His Church.

LOOKING BACK – AND FORWARD
The first eleven verses of Acts 1 span the years from His life on earth to His second coming.

What Jesus did and taught (vv. 1-2). Luke had covered the Lord's life and teachings in his Gospel, and does not add to them here. Jesus Christ is God. He became a human being, identifying with us. His life was spotless, His teachings superb.

Christ's death on a cross (v. 3). The King James version says 'his passion'. At the cross 'God was reconciling the world to himself in Christ' (2 Cor. 5:19). Have you ever said, 'Thank you, Lord, for dying for me'?

His resurrection (v. 3). What a relief! He did not remain dead. Read Romans 6:1-11 for the thrilling implications. Use modern translations for new insights.

His promise of the Holy Spirit (vv. 4-5). The 'Trinity' is the name we use for the three-in-one God. The three persons are all mentioned in these verses: The Father, the Son (who is speaking), and the Holy Spirit.

His silence concerning irrelevant matters (vv. 6-7). The disciples mistakenly expected Him to set Israel free from Roman rule.

His great commission (v. 8). Matthew 28:19-20 also makes plain our Master's clear command to let the whole world know about Him.

His ascension (v. 9). The time came for Him to return to the glory He had left. The disciples saw Him for the last time as He vanished from their sight into a cloud. If He had not gone who, on earth, could now enjoy His company?

His promised return (vv. 10-11). His return is certain. When? We do not know.

FIRST THINGS FIRST
In verses 12-26, the final physical link with Jesus is broken and His followers settle down to the business at hand. Primarily, frequent meetings for prayer keep them in touch with God, and set the pattern for future activity.

One important matter demands their attention. Judas, one of the original twelve apostles, had died in tragic circumstances. A replacement must be found. Following prayer for guidance, Matthias is added to the group of apostles.

The ground is now ready. The building of the church can begin.

STUDY 2
ONENESS THROUGH THE HOLY SPIRIT

QUESTIONS

DAY 1   Acts 2:1-4.
a) Who were involved?

b) What did they: hear? see? do?
blowing of wind - violent
tongues of fire

DAY 2   Acts 2:1-13.
In your thoughts, fly back to that day in Jerusalem. How would you have felt if you had been one of:
a) Jesus' followers, verses 1-4? *in the present overwhelmed,*

b) The Jews, verses 5-12?
amazed - wonderful to be understood / to understand

c) Those in verse 13?
out of it?

DAY 3   Acts 2:14-17; 22-24; 32-33; 36.
a) From today's verses find references to God (the Father), Jesus Christ (His Son), and the Holy Spirit, in Peter's sermon.
v.16 - God said holy spirit   v.22 God through Jesus the man.   v.36 - God making Jesus Christ

b) Is the Lord the main topic of the sermons you usually hear? You will find Peter's whole speech (Acts 2:14-36) interesting reading in a paraphrase (e.g. The Living Bible).

DAY 4   Acts 2:37-39.
a) When Christ is talked about today, do the listeners react as in verse 37? Why? or Why not?

QUESTIONS (cont.)

b) What precedes forgiveness of sins (see also Acts 3:19; 5:31)?

repentance

c) Who can be forgiven?

v. 39 - you, children & all for off.   Acts 10:34-35

DAY 5   Exodus 32:19-28; Acts 2:40-41.
a) When the Israelites disobeyed God as Moses was receiving the Ten Commandments, how many died?

b) When the Holy Spirit was poured out, how many received eternal life?

c) How does this illustrate 2 Corinthians 3:6?

"He has made us competent as ministers of a new covenant — not of the letter but of the spirit for the letter kills but the spirit gives life."

DAY 6   Acts 2:42-47; Galatians 5:22-23; Luke 24:52-53.
a) What were the characteristic features of the early Christians?

b) Which of these are true in your life?

DAY 7   Acts 2:38, 42, 46, 47.
a) They experienced a joyful oneness. Who or what bound them together?

b) What can you do to break down barriers in your world?

NOTES

Acts Two. What an exciting chapter! Scholars have written thousands of words on the events recorded here. We have space for only a few. So, in a nutshell ... The Holy Spirit is one of the three persons in the eternally existent Godhead. He did not have His beginning on the Day of Pentecost, any more than God's Son came into being on the first Christmas Day. The Holy Spirit, the Son, and the Father comprise the eternal God, without beginning and without end.

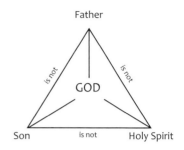

To mark the momentous occasion of the Church's beginning, three symbols were given: a sound like wind (loud enough to bring men running), the appearance of fiery looking tongues, and the use of languages not known to the men who spoke them. Their topic? The wonderful works of God!

The confused reaction of the crowd led to Peter's masterly explanation. His speech became the first Christian sermon, and truly gave Jesus Christ the honour which is His right as Lord. This is how Christ was preached on the Church's birthday.

Remember that the early Christians were all Jews. If not born Jews, they were proselytes (converts) to Judaism. Peter's audience, too, were Jews. To base his arguments on the Old Testament was quite natural, as they all knew this well. He suited his preaching to his listeners. He built on their existing knowledge. He argued logically that Jesus was their Messiah-Christ, that His death and resurrection formed an essential part of history, and that all people were in need of the forgiveness He offered. He quoted from the Old Testament: Joel 2:28-32; Psalm 16:8-11; Psalm 132:11; 2 Samuel 7:12-13; Psalm 110:1.

As events unfolded in the years ahead, Christian teaching included other truths, but Peter's message on that occasion contained all the necessary ingredients for that audience. And it brought results.

Verses 41 and 42 contain in miniature the fundamentals of church life. What follows?

Indwelt by Jesus Christ's Holy Spirit and making Him the centre of life, Christians found themselves drawn to each other in a love not known before. No wonder many new converts joined the church every day!

STUDY 3
POWER IN JESUS' NAME

QUESTIONS

DAY 1 Acts 3:1; 1:14; 2:42; Luke 24:53.
a) Share what you know of good results of prayer meetings.
Communal, informal - frequent & formal, committed continually at the temple praying

b) Some people seem reluctant to join others for prayer. Can you suggest a remedy for this problem?

DAY 2 Acts 3:2-4; Luke 18:18-23; 19:8.
a) Why would a crippled man choose God's house as the place to beg?
Commanded to give as an act of worship so good place to beg

b) In what practical ways can we, in our situation, help people less fortunate than ourselves?

DAY 3 Acts 3:5; 4:22.
a) If you were that forty-year-old man, what would you want Peter and John to do for you?

b) What was the most he expected?
money.

DAY 4 Acts 3:6-8.
a) Rewrite today's verses in about ten words. Now describe the event in one word.
Healing.

b) What does Ephesians 3:20-21 tell us that God can do? Do you believe this?
more than we can ask/imagine.

QUESTIONS (cont.)

DAY 5 Acts 3:8-11; Colossians 3:16-17.
a) To whom did the lame man give the credit for his healing?

b) When should we give thanks to God? Do we forget sometimes? Think about Luke 17:16-18; Philippians 4:6, 7; 1 Thessalonians 5:16-18.

DAY 6 Acts 3:12-16, 19, 26. Read verses 12-26 if you have time.
a) What did Peter accuse the people of doing? Are we free of any blame?

thinking that Peter's godliness had healed

b) What did Peter urge them to do?

faith in Christ – repent

DAY 7 Acts 4:8-12; Philippians 2:5-11.
a) Can you detect any self-satisfaction in Peter's behaviour?

No – just confidence in Jesus.

b) Who will be excused from honouring Jesus Christ as 'Lord'?

every tongue confess

c) Using verses 6 and 16 as keys, unlock the whole of chapter 3 as you read through it again. What have you learned about the Name of Jesus?

power of name & faith that comes through him

NOTES

Chapter three follows a similar pattern to chapter two. First, a miracle takes place. Then Peter grasps the opportunity to talk about Jesus to the Jewish crowd.

MIRACLE THROUGH JESUS' NAME
Why did Joseph and Mary choose 'Jesus' as the name for God's son? Simply because God's angel told them to (Matt. 1:20-21). 'Jesus' means 'Saviour'.

While many Jewish men bore the name Jesus, there was only one Jesus Christ of Nazareth. To avoid any mistake as to the power behind the healing miracle, Peter identified Him: 'In the name of Jesus Christ of Nazareth, walk' (v. 6), and repeated the phrase the next day (4:10). The power-producing name belonged to one person only.

To show that this was no imaginary cure from an imagined illness, Luke spelled out the details. Here we detect the medical interest of Doctor Luke, the author (Col. 4:14). The man had been crippled from birth (v. 2), his feet and ankle bones grew strong at once (v. 7), and he started jumping and walking (v. 8). (Try walking after even a few months in bed!) This man, over forty years old, had never walked.

GROUNDS FOR FAITH IN JESUS' NAME
We who look back after two thousand years, may have little difficulty in understanding who Jesus was. The Old and New Testaments together form our Bible. We read prophecies and their fulfilment between the covers of the one book. But to many Israelites living in the Acts period, Jesus of Nazareth meant nothing. Peter set out to convince his fellow-Israelites that Jesus was their Messiah. He placed facts before them: facts of Jesus' life and death, their part in those events, and Scriptures foretelling the coming of the Messiah.

v. 13	The God of our fathers gave glory to Jesus. You rejected Him.
v. 14	You rejected the Holy and Just One, and chose a murderer instead.
v. 15	You killed the source of life. God raised Him from the dead.
vv. 17-18	You acted in ignorance. God overruled your ignorance, using it to fulfil the prophecies (Isa. 53).
vv. 22-23	God said through Moses He would send a prophet who must be obeyed (Deut. 18:15, 18, 19). Jesus was that prophet.
v. 24	All the prophets spoke about these days.
v. 25	You are the children of those prophets, and included in the covenant with Abraham. (Gen. 22:18).
v. 26	God raised Jesus from the dead. It was to you Israelites first that God sent Him with blessing as you turn away from wickedness.

At this point Peter is interrupted. He picks up the theme again next day.

STUDY 4
FIRST PERSECUTION PRODUCES BOLDNESS

QUESTIONS

DAY 1   Acts 4:1-4; 23:8.
a) Did the Sadducees and others have good reason for being annoyed? Why?

b) When we talk about Jesus Christ, what opposition may come our way?

DAY 2   Acts 4:5-12; Psalm 118:22.
a) In today's reading, find references to the three Persons of the Trinity (God the Father, Jesus Christ and the Holy Spirit).

b) Who is the 'stone', rejected by the Jews, but honoured by God?

c) How many religions lead to salvation?

DAY 3   Acts 4:13-17; Luke 12:11-12.
a) Describe the dilemma of the officials.

b) How was Jesus' promise in Luke 12 fulfilled for Peter and John?

DAY 4   Acts 4:18-22; 1:8; Luke 22:54-62; 1 Peter 2:13-15.
a) Should Peter and John have obeyed the rulers' orders in verse 18?

QUESTIONS (cont.)

b) Compare Peter's actions in Luke 22 with those in Acts 4.

DAY 5   Acts 4:23-31, 33; Psalm 2:1-2.
a) How were the other believers affected by Peter and John's experience?

b) Is it true to say that God answered their prayer of verse 29?

DAY 6   Acts 4:32-37; John 13:34-35.
a) What connection is there between today's two readings?

b) Discuss how we can follow these teachings today.

DAY 7
a) What results, good or bad, sprang from the lame man's healing?

b) Which verses in Acts 4 show the courage of the believers?

c) Keep your eyes and ears open for news of modern-day courageous Christians.

NOTES

IMAGINARY CORRESPONDENCE WITH PETER

Dear Peter,
   Greetings from the Twenty-first Century! Reading about you and your adventures, we are puzzled. Peter, you are an enigma! How could you deny your Lord? Then after you'd been so afraid, what brought about such a complete change in you? Your boldness challenges us. Tell us your secret.
   Yours sincerely,
   Twenty-first Century Readers.

Dear Scattered Friends,
Your questions do not surprise me. I, too, am amazed when I look back. To begin with, why did Jesus choose me, an ordinary fisherman? Then, possessing the honour of apostleship under the Son of God, why did I fail Him so often! The only explanation I can give is that I, unstable, impetuous Simon Peter, was trusting in my own ability. My life in those days was simply the life of Peter, self-confident Peter.
   Why the change? One powerful factor was the Lord's forgiveness. No matter how deep His disappointment in me, my repentance was followed by His loving forgiveness. Even after I had denied Him (three times!) He took me back, and actually told me that a special work awaited me.
   The BIG influence on all of us was His resurrection. We couldn't grasp the possibility even when He told us in advance, so we were shattered and miserable while He lay in the tomb. Imagine our amazement when He came back to us ... alive! He was risen indeed! We saw Him several times; He talked with us; finally we watched Him ascend to the Father. From then on the resurrection pulsed through all our preaching.
   Then, too, we clung to His promise of constant nearness (Matt. 28:20). With great anticipation we waited for the promised Holy Spirit, for only through Him could our Lord live in us. Precious though Jesus' nearness had been, this was far surpassed by His indwelling. From the Day of Pentecost on, every Christian could enjoy the blessing of His presence all the time.
   To sum up, three factors changed me from insecurity to boldness:

1. Christ's saving forgiveness (Acts 3:19; 4:12);
2. His resurrection (Acts 4:2, 10, 33);
3. His Holy Spirit (Acts 4:8, 31).

I hope you, too, are living by His power.
Yours sincerely in Jesus Christ,
Peter.
P.S. Be sure to read carefully my First Century letters in the New Testament. The Holy Spirit had you in mind when He prompted me to write them.

STUDY 5
WILLING TO SUFFER

QUESTIONS

DAY 1   Acts 4:36–5:6.
a) Following the positive illustration of early church life in Acts 4:32-37, we now read of a negative illustration. What did Barnabas and Ananias have in common?

b) How did the two men differ?

DAY 2   Acts 5:7-11.
From this whole vivid story, what have you learned about God's attitude to hypocrisy?

DAY 3   Acts 5:12-16; Mark 16:15-18; Acts 1:8.
a) In one word describe the church of that time.

b) In the verses in Mark, Jesus had made certain promises to the apostles. Which promises were now coming true?

c) What part of Acts 1:8 was being fulfilled?

DAY 4   Acts 5:17-21a.
a) What prompted the Sadducees to arrest the apostles again?

b) Keeping in mind what happened to them in Acts 4, would you have joined them in the first part of 5:21?

QUESTIONS (cont.)

DAY 5   Acts 5:21b-32; Philippians 2:9.
a) Find the link between today's two readings.

b) In replying to the high priest (5:29-32), what topic does Peter make a lot of?

c) Memorise Acts 5:29.

DAY 6   Acts 5:33-40; 22:3.
How did one man, Gamaliel, succeed in influencing the whole Jewish council?

DAY 7   Acts 5:40-42; Romans 8:17; 1 Peter 3:8-17.
Discuss the connection between suffering and happiness, first from a worldly point of view, and then from a Christian viewpoint.

NOTES

A newspaper reporter comments: Conflicting reports continue to flow in over the bizarre events involving the followers of Jesus. These men still maintain that their leader appeared several times after being crucified and buried. To this date, his body has not been found. Trickery? Or truth?

Reliable sources state that a man called Peter (and others) performs miraculous healings through the name of Jesus. A more melancholy report cites the sudden death of a man and his wife for as slight an offence as a white lie. The Jesus people say such an event teaches honesty, and purifies their sect.

In spite of being treated harshly, the group displays surprisingly good spirits. Certainly a movement worth watching!

A High Priest reflects: Just when I think I have these fanatics where I want them, they come to light again, as brazen as ever. Their leading 'apostle' (an ex-fisherman named Peter) acts like a man possessed by some strange power. What vexes me most is their obnoxious, persistent preaching that Jesus rose from the dead. We Sadducees know the absurdity of the dead-raised-to-life theory. Why can't we shatter this ridiculous rumour once and for all? Punishment seemingly has no effect. In fact, they appear actually to enjoy their pain. What am I to do? What about my popularity if I act harshly? And yet it's such a politically dangerous movement....

A new convert testifies: This time last week my wife and I were as opposed to 'The Way' as anyone. Our neighbours often told us of their faith in Jesus as the Messiah. But we would have none of it. Then, quite by chance, we saw a miraculous healing ... right before our eyes! Next, the Sadducees imprisoned the apostles, and an angel set them free. When we finally listened to their teaching, we were convinced of its truth. We saw that we needed forgiveness. We expect that troubles will come as we follow Jesus Christ. Even so, we gladly align ourselves with Him and His people.

An apostle writes: We twelve feel that the tragedy of Ananias and Sapphira has ushered us into a new phase. We had been thrilled to see numbers growing. The believers were practising love and fellowship and generosity. Now we are aware of the dangers that can emerge from inside our group. Let's hope we have learned our lesson, and will avoid further perils in our midst.

Life has developed into a pattern of persecution, suffering, joy, preaching and prayer. We are under tremendous pressures of work for Jesus, work which brings deep satisfaction. Peter and John and the rest of us agree that we are living in the most exciting days of our lives.

STUDY 6
THE FIRST MARTYR FORGIVES

QUESTIONS

DAY 1   Acts 6:1-4.
a) Differences in languages and customs can be blamed for many needless quarrels. What problems arose in the early church?

b) Are you aware of potential trouble spots in your situation?

c) What type of person was needed for the mundane work of serving tables?

DAY 2   Acts 6:2-4,6-7; Matthew 10:1-4.
a) Describe the role of that special group, the apostles.

b) If prayer and scriptural preaching increase, what results can we expect?

DAY 3   Acts 6:8-15.
a) Complete the steps taken by Stephen's enemies:
Step 1 (v. 9)   They argued with him.

Step 2 (v. 11)   ....

Step 3 (v. 12)   ....

Step 4 (vv. 13-14)   ....

b) What was Stephen's reaction in verse 15?

QUESTIONS (cont.)

DAY 4   In Acts 7:2-50 Stephen recounts a long period of the history of God's chosen people (Jews, or Hebrews, or Israelites, or Children of Israel, or the 'Fathers').

	Where recorded in O.T.	Main Subject
Acts 7:2-8	Genesis 11:27–25:11	Abraham (or Abram)
Acts 7:9-19	Genesis 25:19–50:26	Jacob (or Israel)
Acts 7:20-46	Exodus, Leviticus, Numbers, Deuteronomy	Moses
Acts 7:47-50	1 Kings chapters 5–8	Solomon's Temple

Stephen has been accused of speaking against the Temple. What is the point of his answer in Acts 7:44-50?

DAY 5   Acts 7:51-53.
   a) What three accusations did Stephen bring against his accusers?

   b) What lessons should we be learning from Stephen's accusers?

DAY 6   Acts 7:54-56; Mark 14:62.
   a) Faced with the truth about their ancestors and themselves, did the Council show a natural reaction? Do you find that the truth sometimes hurts?

   b) Although surrounded by angry faces, Stephen saw a glorious sight. How would this have affected him?

DAY 7   Acts 7:57-8:2; Luke 23:34.
   All we know of Stephen is found in this week's readings. In what way are you challenged by his submission to Christ as Lord?

NOTES

STEPHEN, ONE OF THE CHURCH'S FIRST OFFICE-BEARERS. The complaint over daily distribution ... was it just a grievance? Or unfounded grumbling? We are not told. The number of disciples had reached many thousands; large numbers of widows would be included. Their problem led to the selection of seven men with appropriate gifts, and, it seems, all from the complaining party! The apostles were not too proud for menial work. The situation required careful understanding of each man's role, and right priorities in the use of his time. Of the seven chosen helpers, Stephen and Philip became preachers. Luke highlights Stephen's activities here, showing the right man in the right place at the right time. Church growth later demanded more sorting out of tasks, principles dealt with further on in the New Testament.

STEPHEN, THE BIBLE TEACHER. Stephen meets lies and half-truths about himself with a factual recital of Old Testament history and its application. Familiar with his Bible, he stands on solid historical ground. His speech contains more than history, however. It shows Christianity as the 'intended goal of the whole history of the Hebrews' (Metzger). As the first Christian apologist, Stephen sets an example: know your Bible, and be prepared to explain your beliefs (1 Pet. 3:15). Hearsay, opinion, and experience can never replace the truth of God's Word.

STEPHEN, THE FIRST CHRISTIAN MARTYR. 'In this day and age there may be some Christians who will be called, like Stephen, to lay down their lives for Jesus' sake. Hostility is emerging, more vicious, more furious, more enraged on every side. We may face in our own day a tremendous outpouring of the hostility of depraved hearts against the message of Jesus Christ and a persecution of its bearers. May God grant that, like Stephen, we will be faithful unto death' (Ray Stedman in *Birth of the Body*).

'Faithful witness to the Lord Jesus Christ can only be given by those who are willing to be martyrs. Deep-rooted conviction, rather than false bravado, produces heroes. If we have that kind of faith in the Lord Jesus Christ, we need never fear what we will do in the time of stress. A faithful witness will make a faithful martyr! Revelation 2:13' (W. S. Lasor in *Church Alive*).

STEPHEN, THE FORGIVER. In our first five studies, Christ's Lordship is seen in: Faith in the Saviour; Unity in the Spirit; Power in Jesus' name; Boldness amid Persecution; Willingness to Suffer. To that list we should add Forgiveness. Not once has revenge been contemplated. Although the Stephen story does not use the word 'forgiveness', its essence pervades the final verses of Acts 7. To round off this week's study look thoughtfully at: Matthew 5:43-48; 6:7-15; Ephesians 4:32; 1 John 2:12.

STUDY 7
THE FIRST OUTWARD MOVE

QUESTIONS

DAY 1   Acts 7:57–8:3; Philippians 3:4-6.
a) How do these verses show Saul as a sincere young man?

b) Is it enough to be sincere in what we believe?

DAY 2   Acts 8:1-8.
Discuss this statement:
'Persecution against the church never need hinder its expansion'.

DAY 3   Acts 8:9-24; 2:38.
a) How had Simon won his popularity?

b) What did his baptism mean to him?

DAY 4   Acts 8:1, 14-25.
When Peter and John went to Samaria, what did they accomplish?

DAY 5   Acts 6:5-6; 8:4-13, 26-40.
a) What was Philip's first role in the church?

b) What did Philip do in Samaria?

c) Consider the social differences between Philip and the Ethiopian. How were the barriers broken down?

QUESTIONS (cont.)

DAY 6 Acts 8:26-40; Isaiah 53:7-8.
a) Who was the subject of the prophecy the Ethiopian was reading?

b) Who organised the 'coincidence' that brought the two men together? Genesis 24 is an example in the Old Testament of a meeting by 'coincidence'.

DAY 7 Acts 8
a) Consult a map and find the places referred to in this chapter. (First Century Ethiopia was directly south of Egypt, whereas modern Ethiopia is located to the south east.)

b) How do the events in Acts 8 relate to Acts 1:8?

NOTES

THE CHURCH so far has been concentrated in and around Jerusalem. According to Acts 1:8 the next phase is an outward push. Not that the apostles held discussions to plan the moves, the Lord of the church held control. It was His strategy that took His witnesses out to new locations. He used persecution to move large numbers out; Peter and John were sent out to train the church; obedience to an angel's directions moved Philip out and a seeking soul from Ethiopia became a witness on his way home.

SAUL (PAUL) enters the scene. Who is he? A young aristocrat from wealthy Tarsus (Acts 21:39); of a Benjamite family (Rom. 11:1); honoured with Roman citizenship (Acts 22:25-28); highly educated (Acts 22:3); a passionate supporter of Jewish law (Acts 26:5); a Pharisee who hated Christianity (Acts 26:5, 9-11); an approving eyewitness of Stephen's death (which would be hard to forget). Paul's story and his letters fill at least two thirds of the remaining New Testament pages.

SIMON (SIMON MAGUS) became a baptised believer, part of the Christian group. Simon said and did some of the 'right' things, but showed no evidence of true conversion. He had always been interested in his own power and prestige, and continued to covet untold power for his own satisfaction. Beware of false Christianity! The word 'simony' has been attached to the sin of trying to buy religious power with money.

PETER AND JOHN, two of the twelve apostles, were specially ordained by Jesus 'that they might be with him and that he might send them forth' (Mark 3:14). Both figure prominently in the Gospels and in these early chapters of Acts. Writings from both men form part of our Bible, though they began life as fishermen. Who knows what the Holy Spirit has in store for any yielded person!

PHILIP, THE EVANGELIST (not to be confused with Philip the apostle), first appears in Acts 6. Acts 8 shows him as (1) broadminded (willing to go to the despised Samaritans), (2) Spirit-led (obedient to the Lord's directions), and (3) a Bible preacher (to city crowds and to a solitary traveller). About twenty years later, author Luke visited Philip's home (Acts 21:8-10). We can imagine long conversations about early events.

THE ETHIOPIAN EUNUCH was treasurer to the Queen Mother. The king, being regarded as a god, was not to be worried with secular matters. The eunuch was evidently a proselyte (a Gentile convert to the Jewish faith). We would like to know the how and why of that conversion, but God keeps it secret. His long journey to Jerusalem had not brought heart satisfaction. The prophecy he read remained a mystery until, joy of joys, he happened to meet Philip. Result: he went on his way rejoicing! And no wonder. He now knew Jesus Christ!

Meanwhile, back in Jerusalem … to be continued next week.

STUDY 8
AN ENEMY BECOMES AN ALLY

QUESTIONS

DAY 1   Acts 9:1-2; Acts 26:9-11.
a) Had we known Saul at that time, how would we have felt towards him?

b) Saul seemed unlikely to become a Christian. Do you know someone as 'impossible' as Saul? What are you doing for that person?

DAY 2   Acts 9:3-9.
Complete these sentences:
a) Saul learned that in attacking the Christians he was really
....

b) Saul suddenly changed from being aggressive and giving orders to ....

DAY 3   Acts 9:10-19.
a) What did the Lord reveal to Ananias about Saul's future? Link the following scriptures with this question: Romans 1:13-15; Acts 13:46-48; Acts 26:1, 2, 32; 2 Corinthians 11:23-29.

b) Discuss the place of Judas and Ananias in Saul's conversion.

DAY 4   Acts 9:19-24.
Compare Saul's activities in Damascus with what he had planned. (Note that a long period in Arabia probably comes between vv. 21 and 22. See Gal. 1:15-17.)

QUESTIONS (cont.)

DAY 5   Acts 9:25-31; 1 John 3:14.
a) Becoming a Christian may bring a person new enemies and new friends. Saul met both opposition and loving fellowship. How did certain Christians show their oneness with him?

b) What does verse 31b teach us about two keys to church growth?

DAY 6   Acts 9:32-35.
a) Who healed Aeneas?

b) How did the incident affect the local people?
(The modern airport outside Tel Aviv is at the ancient town of Lydda, now known as Lod.)

DAY 7   Acts 9:36-43.
a) What role did Dorcas (Tabitha) play in the Joppa church?

b) How did this incident affect the local people?

c) Could your community benefit from some Dorcases today?

NOTES

Saul is furious with the Christians. He obtains letters from the High Priest granting him authority to capture Christians in Damascus. He and his party approach the city. The road is drenched with heat and light from the noon sun. The scene is set for a miraculous conversion. A brilliant light, brighter than the midday sun, envelops the group of men, who fall to the ground.

VOICE: Saul! Saul! Why persecute me? You only hurt yourself by hitting back.
SAUL: Who are you, Lord?
VOICE: I am Jesus, the one you are persecuting.
SAUL: What shall I do, Lord?
VOICE: Stand up and go into the city. There you will be told what to do. I have appeared to you to appoint you as my servant and witness. You are to tell others all that I show you. I will keep you safe from Jews and Gentiles to whom I shall send you. You are to turn them from darkness to light, so they may be forgiven through their faith.

Saul stands up, appears dazed. Unable to see, he is led by the hand into Damascus. He goes without food and water for three days. A believer named Ananias has a vision.

THE LORD: Go to Judas' house and ask for a man named Saul. He is praying and in a vision has seen you come to lay your hands on him to restore his sight.
ANANIAS: But Lord! I have heard about this man's murderous campaign in Jerusalem. Now he has come with authority to arrest your people here.
THE LORD: Go! I have chosen him to serve me. I myself will show him all he must suffer for my sake.

Ananias finds Saul and places his hands on him.

ANANIAS: Brother Saul! The Lord Jesus sent me to you so that you might see again and be filled with the Holy Spirit.

Something like scales falls from Saul's eyes, and he can see again. He is baptised, has a meal and feels strong again. He takes his place among Jesus' followers, and begins to preach that Jesus is the Son of God.

(A condensed account of Saul's conversion, based on Acts 9:1-20; 22:4-16; 26:11-18.)

'Saul was an unusually strong-willed man. And when God goes out to get a strong-willed man, He has to use unusual methods' (W. S. LaSor).

Acts 9 shows the Lord of the church at work in three directions: in winning over an enemy, Saul; in defeating Aeneas' sickness; and in restoring Dorcas to life. Let us not ask why these three were picked out. Remember that all three later died. It is enough to know that God's will, while seeming mysterious to us, is perfect.

STUDY 9
A NON-RACIST GOSPEL

QUESTIONS

DAY 1   Acts 10:1-8, 22-25, 33; 11:3.
Describe Cornelius as a person.

DAY 2   Acts 10:9-16.
Why was the vision given three times? (Refer to Leviticus 11 and Deuteronomy 14 to understand Peter's prejudice about food.)

DAY 3   Acts 10:17-23.
a) What do verses 17 and 19 tell us about Peter's reaction to the vision?

b) Are you ready to obey the Spirit's leading as Peter was?

DAY 4   Acts 10:24-33.
a) In today's reading do you see proof of a radical change in Peter's thinking?

b) In the light of John 3:16 and Revelation 5:9, why should we look on people of all races as of equal value?

DAY 5   Acts 10:34-48.
a) Who was the subject of Peter's talk to the Gentiles that day?

b) God taught Peter a vital truth in Acts 10. What was it?

QUESTIONS (cont.)

c) When was Peter finally, completely convinced (see also Acts 11:17)?

DAY 6   Acts 11:1-18.
a) Is it true to say that all the Jerusalem believers criticised Peter?

b) When God shows you a truth you have not seen before, do you praise Him for it?

DAY 7   Acts 11:19-30.
a) Find at least three ways in which the church at Antioch sets an example that the church today could follow.

b) Do you need to give special heed to any of these points? Be honest!

NOTES

Jesus Christ, Lord of the Church, had been mightily at work. Astonishing growth took place; thousands were converted; the gospel spread out from Jerusalem in widening circles. Acts 1:8 was coming true. Key men won to Christ were being prepared for future ministry. All very exciting!

The church however lacked understanding of the basic fact that God cares for all people. Although filled with the Holy Spirit, they needed to be taught this important truth by that same Holy Spirit. Peter in the forefront of advance, was as slow as anyone to grasp the universality of Christianity. Large chunks of prejudice had to be removed from his thinking. The story in Acts 10 and 11 portrays a great turning point in the history of the church.

Cornelius was a Roman centurion, that is, captain of one hundred men. He would be a man of courage and loyalty. He must have tired of the emptiness and sensuality connected with Roman paganism, and reached out after God. He lived almost as a Jew regarding food and times of prayer. The centurion was a 'God-fearer' but was not a full proselyte to the Jewish religion. He was not circumcised, therefore counted as a Gentile. Cornelius was obedient to the light he had, and God made sure he was led to the place where he could come to know Jesus Christ. The gathering of friends in his house has been described as 'one of the most strategic home Bible classes ever held'.

Caesarea, on the Mediterranean coast, sixty miles north-west of Jerusalem, was the location of the Roman governor of Judea, and base for a substantial army.

PETER AND THE LAW. We should not smugly criticise Peter for his attitude to 'unclean' food. He carefully followed God's Old Testament law. We must understand that the transition from law to grace involved tremendous changes. However, it has been pointed out that his opening words in Acts 10:28 referred only to man's law, not God's. God had not forbidden association with people of other nations.

THE CIRCUMCISION PARTY (11:2). Circumcision was ordained by God to set his people apart under the old covenant (Gen. 17:9-14). From ancient times Israelites looked on the uncircumcised with contempt. Certain Christian Jews who believed the rite should be carried over into the church, were known as the Circumcision Party, or Judaizers. Their disrupting influence had to be faced again and again as the church grew.

Syrian Antioch was noted for sports, culture, scholarship, and low morals. Jerusalem had served as the church's centre; now Antioch has become the springboard for its spread. Remember: God's purpose reaches to the ends of the earth (Acts 1:8).

STUDY 10
THE CHURCH CANNOT BE DESTROYED

QUESTIONS

DAY 1   Acts 12:1-2; Mark 10:35-40.
Discuss the connection between today's two readings.

DAY 2   Acts 12:3-5.
Are these statements true or false?
a) Peter was arrested for plotting against the king.

b) Pending trial, he was allowed out on bail.

c) Humanly speaking, Peter stood no chance of escaping death.

d) The church followed the only possible line of action. Look for news of at least one person going through similar trials for Christ today. Take time to pray.

DAY 3   Acts 12:6-11.
a) How do you account for Peter's calm sleep?

b) How long did it take him to realise what was happening?

DAY 4   Acts 12:12-19.
a) Make a list of those who were surprised at Peter's escape.

QUESTIONS (cont.)

       b) Are you sometimes surprised when God answers your prayers?

DAY 5   1 Peter 4:12-16; John 21:17-19; Acts 4:1-3; 5:17-18, 40-41.
       a) Peter wrote about suffering in his letter. How had he learned such wisdom?

       b) What attitude does he encourage in 1 Peter 4:13? What reward is promised?

       c) Do you pray constantly for someone who suffers more deeply than you?

DAY 6   Acts 12:19-25.
       a) Although Herod was a murderer and a persecutor, his life was not taken for these reasons. Why was he struck down?

       b) While a pompous king was being dealt with, what was taking place out among the people?

DAY 7
       a) Why didn't the infant church die out during its early years?

       b) 'Jesus Christ is Lord!' Describe how Luke highlights this theme in Acts chapters 1-12.

NOTES

About fourteen years since its beginning, the church numbered countless thousands. It was spreading rapidly.

The arrogant King Herod Agrippa I (nephew of the Herod before whom Jesus appeared) instigated a new wave of opposition. For James to become Herod's number one target, we can assume that he had been busy evangelising. James had once asked the Lord for a top position. Now he became 'top' in another sense – he was the first apostle to be martyred.

Carried away with his success over James, and keen to retain his popularity, Herod arrested Peter. If it had not been Passover time, Peter would have been slain at once. Picture Peter, securely guarded and chained, sound asleep. Then imagine the Christians (not all in one place, of course) praying non-stop for him. We wonder how much faith accompanied their prayers, but at least they prayed with amazing results.

The rescuing angel showed a loving concern for Peter. He brought a light, and made sure Peter put on his shoes and coat. Some of us today are used to self-opening doors, but Peter had never seen one before! He thought he was dreaming! Once he got his bearings, he knew where to go – to the home of Christian friends. Sure enough, many were there praying. It seems from verse 17 that the other James (half brother of Jesus) was praying with others in another place.

Predictably, the prisoner's escape caused panic among the guards, and greater anger in Herod. Innocent soldiers died because the vicious king did not believe their story. The tyrant's pompous pride led to the twisted state of mind where he actually believed his own great power made him a god. An account of his tragic death, set down by Luke in Acts 12, is also recorded by the historian, Josephus.

Now look at the vast activity in verses 24 and 25. Every single town hearing the gospel was a victory, every single life given to Christ, a miracle.

The stage had been set for the great outreach to the Gentiles.

> Let the song go round the earth,
> Jesus Christ is Lord!
> Sound his praises, tell his worth,
> Be his name adored;
> Every clime and every tongue
> Join the grand, the glorious song!

ANSWER GUIDE

The following pages contain an Answer Guide. It is recommended that answers to the questions be attempted before turning to this guide. It is only a guide and the answers given should not be treated as exhaustive.

GUIDE TO STUDY 1

DAY 1
- a) All that Jesus did and taught while He was on earth.
- b) Personal.
- c) Luke had received his information from eye witnesses; he had carefully investigated everything; he had written a systematic account.

DAY 2
- a) After His resurrection He met with His disciples many times, talking with them about the Kingdom of God. No doubt there was much more to those meetings than is recorded in the brief references in the Bible.
- b) Personal.
- c) For the promised Holy Spirit.

DAY 3
- a) The Holy Spirit could not come to live in all believers while Jesus was on earth, in the company of only a few at a time. Jesus' rightful place now is in Heaven at God's right hand.
- b) The answer to question two depends on our relationship with Him.

DAY 4
- a) Every single member of the group can be thankful for the coming of the gospel to his or her area.
- b) The Holy Spirit's power.
- c) Encourage a sense of responsibility to one's own town or village, with widening circles to include the whole world.

DAY 5
- a) They would remember the prayer Jesus taught them, and use it as a guide. 'Your kingdom come' would remind them to pray for the spread of His gospel; 'Give us ...' would prompt prayer for needs to be met, etc.
- b) 'The Lord's Prayer' provides an excellent starting point. We should beware of using it slavishly, without meaning (Matt. 6:7).

DAY 6
  a) Warnings against the love of money, and hypocrisy.
  b) He was to be a man who had had close association with the Lord Jesus and His group, and who had seen the risen Lord.

DAY 7
  a) In John 7:5 they did not believe. In Acts 1:14 they are believers. Carefully encourage each person to be sure of his or her position as a 'believer', a true follower of Christ.
  b) The Luke 24 passage is packed full of vital truths which are found again in Acts 1, e.g., Christ's death, resurrection and ascension; the Holy Spirit's coming.

GUIDE TO STUDY 2

DAY 1
  a) It seems that all the believers were there. However, some scholars believe only the twelve apostles were present.
  b) They heard a sound like a strong wind. They saw something that looked like tongues of fire. They talked in languages they themselves did not know.

DAY 2
  a) Excited and exhilarated.
  b) Bewildered, puzzled.
  c) Scoffing, disbelieving of anything supernatural.

DAY 3
  a) Here are a few (you will find others):
     verse 17 Spirit;
     verse 22 Jesus, God;
     verse 33 He (Jesus), the Father, Holy Spirit.
  b) Personal. Answers will depend on preachers.

DAY 4
  a) Seldom, unfortunately. (Possibly because they have heard it all before.)
  b) Repentance.
  c) All who come to God.

DAY 5
  a) Three thousand.
  b) Three thousand.
  c) Those who broke the Law, died; those who received the Spirit, had life.

DAY 6
- a) Teaching; fellowship; breaking of bread ('fellowship meals', possibly the Lord's Supper); prayer; wonderful signs through apostles; sharing; praise to God; respect from outsiders; fruits of the Holy Spirit (Galatians 5:22, 23); worship; corporate thanksgiving.
- b) Personal.

DAY 7
- a) Jesus Christ, by His Spirit, united them.
- b) Variety of answers possible. Jesus Christ is the great barrier breaker.

GUIDE TO STUDY 3

DAY 1
- a) Personal.
- b) This question presents a good opportunity to discuss sharing in prayer. Be sensitive to shyness, etc., in your group members. Praying alone with the Lord is also very important.

DAY 2
- a) God's people would be expected to care about those in need.
- b) Suggestion: By giving money to organisations which help the poor.

DAY 3
- a) To give money, unless we knew their connection with the miracle-working Jesus.
- b) Probably just a gift of money.

DAY 4
- a) Example: Instead of money they gave him healing in Jesus' name. Fantastic! Unbelievable! Life-changing! etc.
- b) Much, much more than we can ask or imagine. Personal.

DAY 5
- a) God.
- b) In all we do or say. Most of us forget, at least sometimes.

DAY 6
- a) They had sent God's Son to His death, preferring a murderer to be set free. Jesus suffered as a result of bearing our sins.
- b) Repent, turn from wicked ways.

DAY 7
    a) No.
    b) No-one. Everyone must ultimately confess that Jesus Christ is Lord.
    c) There is power in the Name of Jesus.

GUIDE TO STUDY 4

DAY 1
    a) With no faith in the possibility of a resurrection, the Sadducees' anger was natural. But all the Jews ought to have known the Old Testament scriptures better.
    b) Personal suggestions.

DAY 2
    a) Verse 8: Holy Spirit; verse 10: Jesus Christ, God; verse 11: Jesus; verse 12: Jesus (implied).
    b) Jesus is the 'stone'.
    c) Jesus Christ alone provides salvation.

DAY 3
    a) They could not deny that the man had been healed through Jesus' power, and were afraid of the news spreading.
    b) The Holy Spirit had obviously given them the right words to say when they stood before the leaders (4:13).

DAY 4
    a) No. They had Jesus' own command to be His witnesses.
    b) Peter had earlier been afraid to confess Christ; now he is bold for Him.

DAY 5
    a) They took the problem to God in prayer, referring to Old Testament scripture.
    b) Yes, verse 33.

DAY 6
    a) Christian love led to sharing.
    b) The basic love principle continues, though its outworking varies according to social and economic conditions.

DAY 7
    a) Some suffering resulted, also much blessing. The message of Christ was spread more widely. The believers faced the cost of obeying Him. And one previously lame man became an exceedingly happy man!

b) Verses 8-13, 19, 20, 33.
c) In your own country, and elsewhere, there are many Christians showing exceptional courage. Encourage your group to pray for these.

GUIDE TO STUDY 5

DAY 1
- a) Both were members of the Church, sold some property, and brought money to the apostles.
- b) Barnabas brought the whole amount. Ananias brought only a part of it, pretending he had brought it all.

DAY 2

God sees and knows all. He expects honesty.
(Emphasise to your group the truth of verses 3-4. The money belonged to them, therefore they had a right to keep it. Their sin was in lying about it.)

DAY 3
- a) Powerful. Successful. Evangelistic. etc.
- b) New people were being saved; sick being healed; miracles.
- c) Witnessing in Judea (out from Jerusalem) Acts 5:16.

DAY 4
- a) Jealousy.
- b) Personal. To join them would take courage.

DAY 5
- a) Acts 5:31 agrees with Philippians 2:9.
- b) The resurrection of Jesus Christ.
- c) Personal.

DAY 6

In his argument he used Theudas and Judas the Galilean, as examples of petty leaders whose causes came to nothing. The new group would likewise disappear if it were not of God. Just in case the apostles were from God, he warned against harming them.

DAY 7

The world's idea of happiness is seeking a life free from pain and suffering, with no troubles. The Christian knows that suffering for Christ leads to honour. Sharing His suffering brings joy.

GUIDE TO STUDY 6

DAY 1
a) Greek-speaking Christians complained that their widows were not being treated fairly. (The early church had some sort of 'dole' or sharing of food.)
b) Answers will depend on situation, and discernment.
c) The seven were to be men, believers, of good reputation, spiritual, wise.

DAY 2
a) Mainly prayer and preaching.
b) The Word of God spreads, and many converts won (Acts 6:7).

DAY 3
a) Argued with him; accused him of blasphemy; arrested him; brought in false witnesses.
b) He maintained a calm, radiant spirit.

DAY 4
God, the Creator, needs no building to live in.

DAY 5
a) They resisted the Holy Spirit; betrayed and murdered the Christ, disobeyed God's Law.
b) We should beware of the trap of blindly following the lines set down by our ancestors, as they were not all on the right track. It is not enough to possess God's Word, we must live by it.

DAY 6
a) Natural? Yes; Spiritual? No.
Personal.
b) Jesus had said He would sit at God's right hand. Stephen saw Him standing there. This would encourage faith that He was ready to give help and strength.

DAY 7
Submission to Christ's Lordship during Stephen's life prepared him for the crucial time of death. He followed Jesus' example in forgiving his murderers.

GUIDE TO STUDY 7

DAY 1
a) He sincerely set out to keep God's law as he understood it. He was not convinced that Jesus was the Messiah (Christ), and acted accordingly.
b) No. It is possible to believe the wrong thing sincerely, as did Saul.

DAY 2
Acts 8 tells how the persecuted church was scattered and yet spread the gospel everywhere. Modern day examples of persecuted believers (not necessarily scattered) provide a challenge as they keep on witnessing for Christ. Sadly in some areas of the world it sometimes appears as if the church has been silenced. Even in these areas we are sometimes surprised at what God is doing. God is sovereign.

DAY 3
a) For a long time he had bewitched the people with magic.
b) His heart was not right before God, therefore baptism was meaningless. Acts 2:38 links repentance (turning from sin) with the outward form of baptism.

DAY 4
They established the Samaritan believers as one body. They dealt with the false Christianity of Simon. They spread the gospel in many villages.

DAY 5
a) He was one of the seven men chosen to distribute food to needy Christians.
b) Proclaimed Christ; did miraculous signs; healed; drove out spirits.
c) Differences: rich, poor; non-Christian, Christian; important official, ordinary man.
By Philip being obedient to the Holy Spirit.

DAY 6
a) Jesus Christ.
b) The angel of the Lord (v. 26), and the Holy Spirit (v. 29).

DAY 7
a) Jerusalem; Judea; Samaria; Gaza; Ethiopia; Azotus (Ashdod); Caesarea. Finding locations on a map reinforces the fact that these were real places, inhabited by real people.
b) In Acts 8 the Holy Spirit leads and empowers Christ's witnesses in the specific places mentioned in 1:8.

GUIDE TO STUDY 8

DAY 1
    a) Some would be afraid of him; angry; feel sorry for him, etc. No doubt some would pray for him, as Stephen did in Acts 7:60.
    b) We should be encouraged to pray for all enemies of Christ. Nothing is too hard for God.

DAY 2
    a) Persecuting the Lord Jesus.
    b) He changed from aggression to humility and submission; and from giving orders, to taking orders and obeying instructions.

DAY 3
    a) Verse 15. Saul was to serve the Lord, and take His message to (1) Gentiles, (2) kings, and (3) people of Israel. He would suffer for Christ's sake. They show that he took the gospel to the groups and individuals mentioned in Acts, and he experienced suffering.
    b) Judas gave him hospitality, Ananias treated him as a brother, took Jesus' message to Saul, and laid hands on him to receive the filling of the Holy Spirit's power. It is interesting that these two men bear the same names as two others whose names were tainted: Judas Iscariot, and the Ananias of Acts 5.

DAY 4
    His plan: to find followers of the Way of the Lord, arrest them, take them bound to Jerusalem.
    What actually happened: He stayed with believers, preached in Jewish synagogues that Jesus is the Son of God, offered convincing proofs that Jesus is the Messiah, drew fierce Jewish opposition.

DAY 5
    a) Some helped him escape from Damascus (perhaps sending him back to Tarsus). In Jerusalem, Barnabas stood with him, explaining the events in Damascus.
    b) The fear (or reverence) of the Lord drives us to keep His commands. The Holy Spirit's help (or comfort) enables us to keep those commands.

DAY 6
    a) Jesus Christ.
    b) Many turned to the Lord.

DAY 7
- a) She spent her time doing good, making clothes for the needy, and generally helping the poor.
- b) Many believed in the Lord.
- c) While the needs vary from place to place, every community needs kind, helpful people.

GUIDE TO STUDY 9

DAY 1
He was a good man, worshipped the true God, gave to the poor, prayed to God, had at least one devout attendant, was respected by the Jews, concerned for friends and relatives, humble, anxious to learn more about God, was not circumcised.

DAY 2
Because Peter was reluctant to obey.

DAY 3
- a) He was puzzled; did not understand its meaning.
- b) Personal.

DAY 4
- a) Being willing to go to Cornelius' house was a big step for Peter.
- b) Christ died for the whole world. No race is excluded from God's love.

DAY 5
- a) Jesus Christ.
- b) That God makes no distinction between Jews and Gentiles.
- c) When Cornelius and his people received the Holy Spirit.

DAY 6
- a) No. Those Jewish Christians who believed that Gentiles should be circumcised were the ones who criticised him.
- b) Personal.

DAY 7
- a) The story is packed with patterns for the church of today: Deliberate preaching of the gospel to Gentiles (v. 20); Jesus referred to as the Lord Jesus (v. 20); Christians taught to remain faithful (v. 23); Consistent teaching by suitable, experienced men (vv. 22-26); They willingly helped fellow-believers in a different area (vv. 28-30).
- b) Personal.

GUIDE TO STUDY 10

DAY 1
    The Lord Jesus warned James about suffering for Him, and it came about in Acts 12.

DAY 2
    a) False.
    b) False.
    c) True.
    d) True.

DAY 3
    a) A clear conscience, and serene trust in God.
    b) He was puzzled until the angel left him in the street.

DAY 4
    a) Peter, Rhoda, the praying Christians, soldiers, Herod.
    b) Personal.

DAY 5
    a) Jesus had taught him, and he learned a great deal from his own experiences.
    b) Rejoicing. Great joy.
    c) Personal.

DAY 6
    a) He tried to usurp honour due to God.
    b) The Word of God was spreading, and many converts were being won to Christ.

DAY 7
    a) It was Christ's Church, the Holy Spirit was active and would not let it die.
    b) Take time to review the whole study course.

GEARED FOR GROWTH BIBLE STUDIES

You can obtain a full list of over 50 'Geared for Growth' studies and order online at:

Our UK Website: www.gearedforgrowth.co.uk

or why not look us up on Facebook.

International enquiries should contact:
wordworldwideinternational@gmail.com

Further information can also be obtained from:

info@gearedforgrowth.co.uk

orders@gearedforgrowth.co.uk

www.christianfocus.com

Find out more about WEC INTERNATIONAL at www.wec-int.org.uk or on Facebook.

Christian Focus Publications
publishes books for all ages

Our mission statement -

STAYING FAITHFUL
In dependence upon God we seek to impact the world through literature faithful to His infallible word, the Bible. Our aim is to ensure that the Lord Jesus Christ is presented as the only hope to obtain forgiveness of sin, live a useful life and look forward to heaven with Him.

REACHING OUT
Christ's last command requires us to reach out to our world with His gospel. We seek to help fulfil that by publishing books that point people towards Jesus and help them develop a Christ-like maturity. We aim to equip all levels of readers for life, work, ministry and mission.

Books in our adult range are published in three imprints:

Christian Focus contains popular works including biographies, commentaries, basic doctrine and Christian living. Our children's books are also published in this imprint.

Mentor focuses on books written at a level suitable for Bible College and seminary students, pastors, and other serious readers. The imprint includes commentaries, doctrinal studies, examination of current issues and church history.

Christian Heritage contains classic writings from the past.

Christian Focus Publications Ltd.
Geanies House, Fearn, Tain, Ross-shire,
IV20 1TW, Scotland, United Kingdom.
info@christianfocus.com
www.christianfocus.com